Except for One
Obscene Brushstroke

Books by Dzvinia Orlowsky

A Handful of Bees
Edge of House
Except for One Obscene Brushstroke

Except for One Obscene Brushstroke

Dzvinia Orlowsky

Dzvinia Orlowsky (handwritten signature)

Carnegie Mellon University Press
Pittsburgh 2003

January 8, 2003

For Walter,

For the heart's greatest intimacies those words have yet to be found, —

"This is all else" —

with humor + heartache, with toughness, vulnerability! some truths claiming to be lies, and some lies striving to be truths —

Hope you like it :)

Love,
Dzv.

Acknowledgments

The following poems, many in different versions, have appeared in the following publications:

Agni: "Elegy"
Mid-Atlantic Review: "I Hope My Daughter Doesn't"
Salamander: "What, Inside These Nights"
Salt Hill Journal: "Clock," "November," "Who Are They Now"
The American Poetry Review: "House Between Water," "Tattoo
  Thoughts," "When Pain Travels Backwards," "You Could Hate Yourself"
The Bitter Oleander: "Under Fluorescent Light"
The Marlboro Review: "In Evil Daddy's Pad"
The Massachusetts Review: "Tornado"
The Onset Review: "Imagine, Then, If We Must"

On-line Publications:
Can We Have Our Ball Back: "At Any Given Moment," "A Voice,"
  "Nocturnal," "Naked, Facing the Mirror,You Recall the Exquisite Animal
You're Not" "Desire," "It Could've Been"
Slope: "Non Legato," "Phone Sex," "The Phone"
The Drunken Boat: "Darwin: From So Simple," "Now Closer,"
  "Letter to Myself"

"Tattoo Thoughts" is included in *Dorothy Parker's Elbow: Tattoos on Writers,
Writers on Tattoos*, Warner Books, 2002.

"House Between Water," "Clock," "When Pain Travels Backwards," and "You
Could Hate Yourself" are included in *New Voices in Ukrainian American
Literature*, Harvard Ukrainian Research Institute, distributed by Harvard
University Press.

My love to Jay Hoffman and our two eaglets, Max and Raisa; to Tessa Sestina
for her artistic input and for lending me her black dress; to my sister, Maria,
for her creative F stops; for my mother who at 82 still wears her high heels; to
Gary Duehr for his invaluable help on these poems at various stages; to
Michael DiPalermo; and to Nancy Mitchell for the gift of her friendship and
her remarkable, infinite insights.

Publication of this book is supported by a grant from
the Pennsylvania Council on the Arts.

PENNSYLVANIA
COUNCIL
ON THE
&
ARTS

Library of Congress Control Number 2002101896
ISBN 0-88748-387-9 Pbk.

10 9 8 7 6 5 4 3 2 1

Contents

I

II

III

For Jay

"Naked I came into the world, but brush
strokes cover me . . ."

—Jeanette Winterson
Art Objects: Essays on Ecstasy and Effrontery

I

November

after Natalka Bilotserkivets

I turn the key, enter my room—
dark corners welcome me.
Muddy taste of rain,
leaves taken into hands,
I could throw my life away
and it'd scarcely make a sound . . .
Shall I go there, where tiles
of light lie in the fields,
to the cobweb's maze,
blood-illuminated words,
to where a stranger removes his gloves,
traces his finger from vein to heart?
Water revives with early snows,
washes fat roots beneath
sidewalks. Uncertain knock,
the glass lamp lit,
I could choke on light
that has yet to pass.

Under Fluorescent Light

much isn't possible–
bloom of a black rose,

dark petals fallen from night,
from a broken vase

held together by our hands.
On my worktable, six flared

velvet capes, underbellies of robins,
muffled hearts, tender

as a body's open borders.
Flowers, actually.

Call them what you wish.

Now Closer

It amazes me the way a man can fall asleep–
the way his chest rises and falls

automatically, as if on life supports,
arms outstretched, one hand slightly curled

as if holding a bird– his penis, lifeless,
like something named then dropped

along the way. And weren't we both awake
minutes ago, loving your weight

pulling me under, dragging me along
what felt like the Atlantic's rocky floor–

just to surface, by myself, on the other side,
wind grazing my small nipples,

something stuck in the sand
only a dog might lick.

Letter to Myself

Once, I confused my own hand
with desire,
once I held it there

until it promised love–
it couldn't possibly get better–
until I realized

I'd rather cry
or take a long bath
alone in the house.

Doesn't it seem
the more thoroughly we wash
the more we stink,

our bodies refuse
to trade in
their own damaged coats–

that even a moment
can take more
that all we've got.

Imagine, Then, if We Must

for Nancy

the letter for which animals wade
the far off creek

under inflated moonlight
along barren October fields.

To the north, a woman sniffs her fingertips
before the city library

pretending to have nursed
an opened book

long after the doors have closed.
It's only a blank piece of paper

turning at her feet.
Imagine the wind, then, if we must,

as postmen
for whom we open bare legs,

unpin our hair.
A painted first O

on a red barn in the middle
of nowhere, Ohio,

heavy pointed weathervane—
Can we say, now,

how our patience began?

House Between Water

For someone else, this thirst
that claims

a single drop's hand-held mirror
facing the sky.

For someone else, this turning
in bed, a downward

burrowing– call it *sleep*,
if only for a few minutes

in that hour when windows open
and all roads end.

For someone else, this silence
like an ill-fitting leather jacket

that will never wear out
no matter how hard time rubs

and burns– this house, its lantern
lifted toward the ocean,

toward towns with families
who wait out each storm,

who secure their yards with gods
and birdhouses,

pinwheels and dwarfs.

What, Inside These Nights

pilfers our meals
while they're still hot,

surprises us with a dead rabbit–
our tiny yard

in its shiftless eyes,
the garden gate opened.

How do we become one
with ourselves

with children older
and stronger than we–

the day folded
as we walk the beach,

the whitened wing
imagined between us

spread tight.
What, if anything,

speaks to me
with my young daughter's

joyful voice
from behind the door

as I step out of the shower,
naked– *all one color.*

Who Are They Now

as we sleep
empty pill bottles at our bed sides

then wake thankful for our belongings
not taken by strangers

by hagglers *how could they*
come to our table who

are they that boil and stir
until the larva rise up

that will not let us kiss
each other's over-forty mouths

while they drive stolen cars
through our meadows

put up *for sale* signs in our yards
walk through the house

shaking their heads *each room so small*
then touch us on the shoulder

just before leaving,
how dare they tempt us into waiting

rocking us in our narrow beds

Nocturnal

They're out there,
he can *feel* them–

as he's shaving,
at a restaurant
ordering steak,

on the verge of coming,
just at the mouth of a tidal river,

blue fish,
bass,
cod.

His young son asleep,
he pulls, instead, a nail
from a small wooden car.

He works late
in the garage,

the sound of crickets
levitating above high grass,

empty waders hanging *ready*
as an astronaut's suit–
sized, silent body.

A Voice

Down the road, a barn's
shingles rot.

Two men pare its roof
with shovels.

Below them, for a moment,
it rains wood.

In their gravity, the day's arguments
tumble back to earth,

accost us as we bend
to scrub our faces,

push our feet into boots.
You who'd have the window opened

must stand naked, and wait.
You who bears the heaviest coat

must ascend ten flights of stairs,
in your sleep, in the dark,

after an alto voice
buzzes you in,

drops its weight like an ax
behind you.

Riding

You collapse like a broken high chair
under your own weight,

the velvet helmet snapped on backwards.
You won't give up

sexy black leather chaps,
despite your ass too big for breeches,

wandering lost past lots and maps,
school committee meetings you forgot

to attend— past hell, its long lines
and hot cafeterias.

Don't think about how little you
ultimately got out of it,

a broken collarbone,
your throat's longest vowel

slammed into earth.
When the recently widowed

lawn-care man asked over the phone
if he could come by

some afternoon to see your horses,
you both knew

he didn't mean the plastic ones
collected in a shoe box,

spilled generously for him
out on the wiped kitchen table.

You've stopped asking why
for some women

a horse's back
comes naturally–

Think of yourself as an anchor.
Think of yourself as something dripping.

typo?

the border without us.

If ...   lready served.

If there is a street, our house might still be there,

If there's a knock, it's a fireman holding a match.

Who took the money and ran?

Who said because of us they at their own hearts?

2.

I'm the one whose skin has drained of color.

I'm the one who said I'd meet you behind the dumpster
at any time on any night.

I lost the key to the room where Mother waits
dressed in her winter coat, the lights turned out,

sent a mousetrap to my grandmother
when she refused to leave behind her furs.

3.

Carry me like a bucket to the field. Empty me fast
near a horse's hoof.

Carry me from bed to bed until I'm warm, until stars
flare at our window,

away from doctors who prescribe *beginners doses*
then go home,

from rooms where I sit fingering a button
like a passenger in a cab to an address the driver doesn't
know

to a room with a man I couldn't turn away from
for whom touching had no approval, the paper work
lost.

4.

And still we hear them through our walls:

rats dragging their tails behind
like heavy wedding trains,

safe under eaves, seemingly drunk,
running erasing running erasing–

5.

Who said the bucking, the fall, the fracture would heal?

Who said it's time for a walk,
for the electric fence to be turned on?

Tap the man in the yard unrolling invisible fence,
tap the dog standing close to his legs.

I am the one who lives in a hive with her tantrum cousin
who bites, claims to clean, to sew–

who doesn't know what to do with soil
once it's been turned.

Elegy

for Ed Hogan,
  for Solomea Pavlychko

Black tree shadows along the paved road
are a safe lake

intertwined with light, a rustling
of leaves undressing,

eager for winter, the cold they won't feel,
anticipating ground.

I'm going nowhere in particular today.
I'm three o'clock passing onto four,

among others whose hearts pump anonymously
at their own doorways, that swell

with excitement, occasional adventure–
packed knife, the apple forgotten.

I was nowhere, last night, in particular,
breathing in my room, dreaming of you–

taking off your jacket, untying your shoes, for you–
making you lighter,

pushing back the water. Today
leaves, scattered from trees,

fall from autumn skies–
from four o'clock passing onto five,

from anything meant to hold or save us.

When Pain Travels Backwards

your body forgets itself, already indiscriminately
a part of the world.

Shattered glass reassembles,
remembers which hand

took the cut, could be counted on.
Miles outside of the city,

blonde pine needles blow sideways
down Blue Hills

ready to startle a horse whose rider
has never ridden before,

whose family waits at the base
of the trail, cameras ready,

full of admiration.
They hold their pee.

But you don't want to think of them or him
or the horse–

Something as big as your heart
faintly sparks at your heels

as you walk around the room.

Feeling all feathery inside,
today you decide

you could have your portrait painted.

In that sweetness, a refrigerator door
opens,

someone you hate has an orgasm.

Theirs Is An Absolute Lack Of

from drawer to table,
kitchen knives– slick, dormant,

placed on their sides.
They stare past the ceiling,

imagine a distant plane
with tiny passengers,

hearts too small to prick
with a needle.

They lack air–
the kind that fattens:

restaurant air,
single chair air,

summer meat air,
that allows them also to grow soft,

bend between fingers,
like too much time on a host's hands,

unpalpable, saltless.
Theirs is an absolute lack of–

rubbed clean,
placed upright

in the dishwasher rack,
forever envying a bread crumb's

savored life
from cut field to mouth,

the stock lily
wrapped for a funeral–

a genital smell
only it knows it has.

At Any Given Moment

God and dog accelerate to the speed of light,
come back as an angry fork.

Daylight falls back to earth
in wide molecular hula swirls.

Did I get this right?

In the meantime, I'm grateful
for the day's abrupt, early spring,

my own luminous skin
freed from its bomb,

as well as for my dark sunglasses,

not lost– but here, on my table
like a misappropriated cricket

held in place
by soundless gates.

II

Tornado

Downstairs, a frieze of naked women
wearing wide black sombreros
waited to be lit on the bar lamp.

I wanted to free them,
to break the glass on the framed
photograph next to them

a white woman kissing a black man.
It looked like she was eating him.
I couldn't swallow for days.

Mother placed it near the lamp
to decorate the house with peril,
drove us into the basement

with seven dogs, all strays,
surrounding us– the first sound
of heavy rain,

while upstairs father counted
money and wanted to be left alone.
Enough for groceries is all he cared.

Sometimes a day or two later,
we'd learn a tornado did pass
small as a bottle

unevenly parting the tips of fields.
Why did she insist
on plugging her ears,

sending father outside
to untie our horse,
lead him into the stall?

She'd wait for something
like a gunshot,
thunder,

or lightning,
no breaths in between,
then lead us out,

saved, a family—
wait for him to come back
from new damp grass.

How did we sleep through the rest—
the almost always
ravaged home,

father's bar in the basement *open*,
flies in the fake ice cubes
looking so poor?

o the Keys

d feast on nothing–
ey stems, a second course
se as mouse knuckles,
horse and rider on my gold
n bracelet banging my thin wrist
as I cut with my knife, politely,
in short, swift strokes.
They scored our posture.
A white linen napkin
covered my lap.

The judges skipped the bathing suit part,
scrapped the talent show,
most of us had none.
(Why embarrass the county?)
Intelligence, however,
would have to speak for itself,
excited by the mike. In the background,
cowboys played donkey basketball
and a hot car prepared
to go up in smoke.

"Who" one judge asked, *"has been
the most influential person in your life?"*
Even now I can feel my parents
squeeze each other's hand,
straighten their backs,
tall in their seats, eyes moist.
Each would be happy for the other.
I answered "Professor Ruwinsky,
my piano teacher" to a hush
in the bleachers, my parents
embarrassed, disappointed,
fading into a blotch.

I don't know why I said his name,
remembering only the clouded
wet spot that I left behind

on the piano bench,
(my skirt too short),

the silence as I stood there,
in horror, hiding my breasts
behind sheet music.
He looked down, long,
quiet as a pharmacist.

I wonder if after I left
he turned to face the conservatory windows,
discreetly dropped his pants–
and if, afterwards, he looked carefully
at his hands that just minutes ago
played sad, deep into the keys–
Maybe he felt peace.

That afternoon we made headlines:
*Three Classy Lassies Crowned
at County Fair*, a photograph of us
on the back of a rented red convertible,
waving slowly to emptying bleachers,
race track grit caught in our teeth.
Honey Bee Queen and Alternates:
a blonde, the winner, who loved
only her parents,
myself, first runner up,

and the second runner up
who like a gust from the cow pavilion
rose up out of nowhere,
the one who if either of us
couldn't make it, if, God forbid,
something went wrong
and one of us died,
would go to State.

from Brunswick, Ohio, while outside fields turn glossy

with ice and in the next room my father
dying– promising, after the morphine takes hold,

to wait for all of us, somewhere, in heaven.
I hope my daughter doesn't become scared

of birds, angry creatures of vast acres,
affordable on the outskirts of town,

holding a metal trash can lid like a shield
as they graze past her. I hope she realizes how

quickly her two-cylinder tractor cuts the grass down,
how her large concentric circles only get smaller.

I hope, like me, she never ties the clothesline around her
                                                            neck
just to see what would happen, then jumps from a limb

wears the cut behind her left ear like her first real secret
to bed for a week.

I hope my daughter doesn't grow up thinking her body's
                                                    childlike
except for one obscene brushstroke,

but that she'll pull that first tongue that enters her
deeper– her head falling slowly back,

eyes closed, and will let stars be stars, unnamed,
above their parked car. Who was the man, disgruntled,

who jerked the car door open, pulled me out of the front
                                                                    seat,
gun to my cheek, calling me *Kathy?*

I hope she doesn't take on God too young,
like the one that caused the kitchen light switch

to spark and catch the wallpaper on fire
or sent down the small plane

killing the last of the town's seamstress's three red
                                                        headed sons,
the other two already dead– one to heroin,

the other in a car accident–
leaving her with an alcoholic husband, a sewing ma-
chine,

and a recent litter of puppies to give away.
I hope I believe whatever my daughter

tries to hand me.
I hope my daughter doesn't grow up thinking

she wants to stay, for her mother to live forever,
and decides toward her life to run away

and does it well– not like a friend and I tried to, once,
dressed in short tank tops and cotton flowered skirts,

hitchhiking to Boulder, Colorado, pulling our skirts up
high above our knees, one car stopped

and pulled off the shoulder, the driver slowly
putting his cigarette out

as both of us turned toward each other, high-fiving,
in disbelief.

Neglected, our garden sprouts rocks.
My son, *so thin*, flies away.
My mother reminds me:
not *all* were executioners.
As a couple, she says,
my husband and I still look sexy
but not 100% in bathing suits.
I want to tell her
her new teeth look good,
that I owe nothing,
that someday my picture too
will fall out of its frame.
But I'm at the back door
when her dog barks—
then, recognizing me,
hurls its body
down the corridor
like a small hatchet.

What Felt Like Music

came in at street level
louder than the washing machine's
lift and bang, my sister's bra
twisting through bleached water,
my *falsies* in a drawer upstairs.
It came in louder
than Mother's *"shit!"*
as she'd open the laundry chute,
dodge our ammunition–
a hammer or rolls
of toilet paper–
heavy mail we called it–
jokes that ran like lighter fluid
between us before any
of us knew how to kiss.
What felt like music
was the sound of a sex-colored,
flame-red Camero parked
in front of the liquor store
revving its engine,
owned (we were told)
by someone whose touch you could
never wash off, like that of the
boy who every Friday,
after school, strategically placed
a stolen lighter in front of his ass.
Anticipating a stunt-artist's flash of fire,
he'd wait until he gathered himself, wait
for his one cashed-in moment of fame
before he'd let himself go,
almost rip.

III

"One's real life is the life one does not lead . . ."

Oscar Wilde

So Smooth

Holding me— both of us lying
against a haystack, she said,
never mind the bruises
around my neck.
never mind the bite
near my ear or the tear
in the waist band
of my pants,
She asked:
Can you remember
if he did anything
between your legs?
Put it somewhere
near or between
your legs?
Sometimes
a teenage boy
could be so smooth
you just couldn't tell.

In Evil Daddy's Pad

He was swishing his long blonde hair,
face down, against my thighs,
we were naked on his water bed,
the first time I knew Wayne.

It must've been something he'd read about
in one of those magazines
that finds itself under a mattress
like a half-pack of cigarettes.

Pretending to swoon, I knew
eventually he'd wipe his tongue
on the fitted sheet
before the taste and feel of me

got to him, made him sick—
before I'd catch him, call him *freak*,
make his neck bulge red,
watch him peel rubber past *bitch*,

past the split-rail fence
running like a Texas border
along his front yard.
The first time Wayne touched me

he said he loved my ash hair,
the way streaks of sunlight fell
around *eyes of a lamb*,
pale eyelashes, all open gasp

letting everyone in.
It made the tiny serpent inside
start to hiss
I could show you a thing or two—

It was different with me
and also different with Rose.
Her last name, too, began with an "O."
She strutted like a Vegas chorus girl

shoulders back, tits like zucchinis
She could dance as though
she were cut in half
a spine that could writhe

until the last bull dropped
He wished he could thank her
for letting him taste her
off his fingertips   he remembered

how, stunned, he moved back
from his steering wheel,
how his friends would never believe
where he'd just been.

Devil With the Blue Dress

On leave from the army,
he'd been places, done things,
once shot a bullet
through a child he thought
was a human grenade.
Now he needs people.
He likes to watch me dance,
sees through me in the black strobe light,
wild and side-pinched against my invisible cage.
I never owned a devil's blue dress
or wanted his one apologetic-right-
thing-gun-shot hand
to find peace with me.
Weeks of night he stood
in the back of the hall
swaying like a tree.
I was too young and stupid
to just let him be;
and cruel enough
to want to know
what they might steal–
his butcher's tongue,
his vein, he'd say,
for the child,
bled open.

Star Land

Divorced only two months,
my first husband's
already at New York's
Plato's Retreat
dancing in a jock strap.
He bubbles open,
watches two women make love,
shyly, in the corner
of the room.

I no longer want his house,
the Sears chandelier flaming
for impatient sex,
the dog left behind,
trained to dump,
if need be,
on the fake oriental rug.

At *Star Land* there are lots
of other bad boys—
leather-vested, bulldogged.
They can't wait to push ahead
to get to their go-carts.
One sneers at me.
The other shakes his skinny
duck-tail, lifts it off his neck.
Her mouth could sure use it.

Closing my eyes, I imagine
the youngest attendant sliding his hand
under my skirt, stroking my leg
like a pelt of fur.

I could never be sexy enough.
Isn't this what my husband vowed to me?
Before slamming the door,
quickly and perfunctorily
flashing me the bird.

Desire

The tiny printed tulips
on your underwear
chirp *okay, cheerful,*
and you admit this is something
you can't seem to shake–
that white layer of skin
you quickly shave your legs
to get to wondering if your husband
would, instead, like you rough–
a slight moustache, maybe– or naked,
at the door, smelling like damp
hydro-seeding in full noon sun,
or its nocturnal animal smell
as he slumps into the room
and the dog, slightly crippled,
makes a slapping sound on the floor
as it lifts to get out of his way.

Think about it: you *do* pocket those extra
hotel complimentary shower caps,
puffed rows lining your bathroom shelf,
little soldiers of lotions and soap
just in case you might have to
travel somewhere– anywhere
overnight (you rarely do),
just you, your poems,
little shampoos
and full-cut underwear.

Alone in your room,
you twist your hair loose,
earrings shimmer like small
chandeliers, bulbs blown,
jack up your calves in heels,
strut across the room
to test your radio antenna.

You're naked before a mirror,
pushing your breasts up,
your body turned slightly to the light

while someone else, caught inside,
pretends not to see or know
like a party invitation that never comes,
or like a son or daughter
who one day without warning
unexpectedly pulls
his or her hand away.

You tell yourself
none of this could possibly
have anything to do with you—
the room's sudden cold,
the sure suicide
just to be seen with you.

In the Wood

She has an ext
pair of nylons
she can't use.
A slip she has
She likes the i

of folding them
into my drawer,
the way I wear
the lambs wool sweater
she gave me

child-size;
It brings out
your eyes.
I'm not lost
in the woods,

but it seems
the harder I run,
the more her hunger
shadows me,
held tongue,

her bathrobe
slides off her shoulders,
onto the floor.
She takes her glasses off,
waits.

I can sense her breath–
like a swimmer's,

slow, on her back–
the uneas
with which

we pretend
we're merely looking out

a window,
or looking up
from books–

interested,
it seems,
in the moment's
only clearing.

You Could Hate Yourself

or you could love yourself
that time his penis didn't rise,
no matter how hard you tried, *worked* at it
like a frantic country wife–

until you fled, in your mind,
to somewhere else,
imagined ringing a telephone operator:
Storm's got the power lines out–

Or when all you pictured was squid,
yards of squid,
each time he stroked your head–
pulled strands of your hair across his lap.

Maybe that's why men always made
that drowning sound fucking you,
why each time, afterwards,
you turned away quickly

from their motionless calm.
Looking back now, you could hate yourself
for the time someone you thought
you wanted to know

walked into the bedroom
lit like a casino
just as you told him *it's over*
because something in the room smelled

like a freezer gone bad,
the room in the walk-up apartment
you thought you wanted because it would help
you to write better–

until you saw the mattress in the middle
of the floor with what looked like bullet holes,
bad accidents mapped across its
bright blue stripes.

Despite this, you wonder what happened
to make you want it so badly, now—
on the stairs,
in the bathroom,

on the seats of an abandoned car—
You could hate yourself
or love yourself every time
you catch yourself in the mirror.

Shocked by *all that fringe,*
truth is: it's your own finger
you're pushing suggestively
into your mouth.

Like on many nights,
you could hate yourself—
or after a moment's pause,
simply roll past yourself like thunder.

In the Rearview Mirror

You don't know what just passed.
It could've been a limousine

or it could've been a hearse.
You take it personally.

Maybe not the limousine.
It'd be ridiculous

for a limousine to take you anywhere
in this small high school town

outside of the city
at your age.

Instead you decide
to drive in broad daylight

with your headlights on
feeling deliciously excessive,

imagine the silver-blue Thunderbird
convertible you still might inherit

although it hasn't been
in the family for years.

Driving in the daylight with headlights on?
Suddenly, in your mind,

they're there again–
those purple *slow procession* flags

flicking on radio antennae.
But *this*, you tell yourself, is winter driving.

Tattoo Thoughts

Because of lightning
on a young waiter's bicep
I lied and said I forgot my sweater,
left my family with our menus,
followed after him, outside,
into the parking lot,

rain coming down,
a few cars, one tree with ugly branches,
clouds tensing into pig shapes
then releasing– I waited for him.
I've thought about the long vine
that like a motorcycle

on an open road
would begin at my shoulder–
I do anything I want–
how words like chrysalis
squirm into blossom,
how a body willingly

takes on its own unnatural blue–
bare winter breasts,
veins like phone wires
beneath my wrist.
Yes, tattoo thoughts.
Yes, better than another small dog.

Once, a woman flinched
when I touched her skin
lightly with my finger.
She must've sensed
the entire small fires in me–
stranger heart,

barbed wire,
Sweet Jesus,
looking buckshot into her eyes–
like I knew she was
going to miss me,
like I'd already left.

Darwin: From So Simple

endless forms: the sticky feelers, subtaceous glands,
oily hands of boys,

fossil strung to fossil every morning someone wakes up,
looks in the mirror, considers lifts, alterations–

How to escape the thick sediment of dreams,
turned face down until you can't breathe, wake startled.

Finches flutter on a sprawl of twigs
and the day's poet struggles

not to write about the barbed hop before flight,
sunflower seeds flung into the wind–

realizing he or she has no place
in the morning's extraordinary abundance.

Consider good intentions, not modified,
that never spread,

unlike one's weight anchored to a favorite chair–
Oh domestic Homeric dune of salt,

the hour lost, unfilled, that flees the room
with its long lizard-like tail.

Who warns the doomed mouse?
The rattlesnake uses its rattle, the cobra flares its frill,

my mind sits crumpled in its wheel chair,
blowing a party horn.

Inheritances of accidental crossings
destroyed by early frosts,

the last union between male and female
creating children who stretch into teenagers–

What instrument measures blood against blood?
The twelfth rose closed and imperfect?

In the laundromat, the long afternoon spins
in large white flapjacks.

A young boy leans up against his girlfriend
in the heat of their skin.

It Could've Been

It could've been– (*don't rush me*)–
at one of those conferences
at big hotels with large over-stuffed
sofas, crackled bars.

We would've shared a room.
We would've moved a heavy stone
over the past which we would've been
trying so hard to write about.

I'd be surprised by the solid curve of your legs.
We would've shared some wine.
Told each other we don't look bad.

I'd catch you in the mirror.
You're too tired for another talk.
I have cramps.
You would've just come out of the shower.

I'd have met you at the bathroom door.
I'd have never kissed another woman before.
I'd be surprised I'm actually doing it.
We'd both be surprised by its weight.

The Phone

For $12.98 it seemed worth it,
a child's black office
telephone.

You believed the advertisement with the girl
pretending earnest conversation
for hours . . .

You sent your money in.

The phone arrived. Rang.

You didn't walk over to answer it because
you bought it specifically
not to have to answer it.

For a moment, you were happy– you were
the good *good* mother who kept
her children home,

although it did bother you
how something faceless
could take on a voice,

address your child, unscrupulously
by his or her first name.

But this wasn't your toy,

it wasn't some squeak
or bell

that called you.

Phone Sex

You weren't going to say this or suggest *that*–
his, or yours.

What you meant to say was *right on*
about when, mostly, about how.

You always knew you wouldn't quite know where it
would go
if he said it first,

or worst, only implied the other
while you were thinking exactly the opposite.

And what if he said, *say it again*, saying *it* again
and you couldn't remember what you said

or how you said it.

You hadn't planned on it coming to this
before it came to that,

making sure you're still alone in the room.

You were only going to ask.
You were only going to call to ask.

Then quickly–

mouth slowly working
the air around the receiver,

you were going to lie.

Naked, Facing the Mirror, You Recall the Exquisite Animal You're Not

Something wooly, rather,
forehead thick as a brick,

fussy, lame tongue
licking the sides of a pill

you cut into two halves.
One for sleep, the other for

it doesn't matter
I'm awake now,

bring on the dead mouse,
the fur ball like a comet

shooting up from your dog's stomach.
Lately, you've given up hunger,

the knife offered for dinner,
the sky's souring buckets of milk,

your past life as a stricken meadow,
pockets of warm water,

lilacs and hummingbirds
garnering frayed scripts.

So duped in love you became all of them:
leaf-climber, tendril-bearer,

unexplained mongrel,
believing all along

you'd suddenly flashed into being
your own character

bare of outlines,
a tangled blank.

Non Legato

It'll come back, the brown moth and its fur-
powdered miniscule prick and huge mirror eyes

some night when it's too hot for common sense
and not quite hot enough for a favorite fantasy

to root and climb its delicate, directional vine.
It'll come back, too, the large doll whose hair I snipped,

the cardboard doll with my head, a stiff photograph
of my face, dressed in a red, blossoming recital dress.

It'll come back and call me old, then hang up.
It'll stand with a drink in one hand and water in the other

and tap its foot until I remember its name. I won't,
the way I can't remember anyone's name, or where

I left what, signed or unsigned. It'll invite friends.
They'll swoop down together over my kitchen sink,

or watch until I step naked out of the bathroom.
I'll swat their bulky air-borne bodies, sinister as gas.

They'll ask if I'd consider having a face-lift,
pretending to be my sister, tell me my hairline looks

like a shallow grave. They'll make me wear gum
on my nose, take a drive in their car– all my teachers

who liked lace-up boots high on my calves.
I know they'll come back, greedy as goats,

chewing on one long flavored piece of string.
I'll talk to no one. Instead, I'll listen

for that single fat possum that dies scratching
each June under my chair, under my floor

its smell, heavy and oily like something I once
brushed on my wrist with a slight glass wand,

just before becoming ill,
feverish in the room's stale air.

I'll turn toward my shadow, lift the moth
between my thumb and finger

like a tiny bow to a sad violin,
the voice that sings non legato, blunted,

blind, that burrows deep inside.

Pietà

I dreamed I'd touched the root of myself
with my tongue's tip.
Hey, get a load of this–

I dreamed men also
went down on themselves
full and warm,

their cocks long
and accessible
as a ticket line

in the otherwise unfilled room.
I dreamed this became a religion
turned to flesh–

accidental cuts rinsed,
tainted bowl of water.
No one questioned this: with all car

windows down,
a field of meadow grass
just beyond the road,

the soul exposed herself, momentarily,
then fled back
to her sober keeper.

Carnegie Mellon Poetry Series

1975
The Living and the Dead, Ann Hayes
In the Face of Descent, T. Alan Broughton

1976
The Week the Dirigible Came, Jay Meek
Full of Lust and Good Usage, Stephen Dunn

1977
How I Escaped from the Labyrinth and Other Poems,
        Philip Dacey
The Lady from the Dark Green Hills, Jim Hall
For Luck: Poems 1962-1977, H. L. Van Brunt
By the Wreckmaster's Cottage, Paula Rankin

1978
New & Selected Poems, James Bertolino
The Sun Fetcher, Michael Dennis Browne
A Circus of Needs, Stephen Dunn
The Crowd Inside, Elizabeth Libbey

1979
Paying Back the Sea, Philip Dow
Swimmer in the Rain, Robert Wallace
Far from Home, T. Alan Broughton
The Room Where Summer Ends, Peter Cooley
No Ordinary World, Mekeel McBride

1980
And the Man Who Was Traveling Never Got Home,
        H. L. Van Brunt
Drawing on the Walls, Jay Meek
The Yellow House on the Corner, Rita Dove
The 8-Step Grapevine, Dara Wier
The Mating Reflex, Jim Hall

1981
A Little Faith, John Skoyles
Augers, Paula Rankin
Walking Home from the Icehouse, Vern Rutsala
Work and Love, Stephen Dunn
The Rote Walker, Mark Jarman

1982
The Granary, Kim R. Stafford
Calling the Dead, C.G. Hanzlicek
Dreams Before Sleep, T. Alan Broughton
Sorting It Out, Anne S. Perlman
Love Is Not a Consolation; It Is a Light, Primus St. John

1983
The Going Under of the Evening Land, Mekeel McBride
Museum, Rita Dove
Air and Salt, Eve Shelnutt
Nightseasons, Peter Cooley

1984
Falling from Stardom, Jonathan Holden
Miracle Mile, Ed Ochester
Girlfriends and Wives, Robert Wallace
Earthly Purposes, Jay Meek
Not Dancing, Stephen Dunn
The Man in the Middle, Gregory Djanikian
A Heart Out of This World, David James
All You Have in Common, Dara Wier

1985
Smoke from the Fires, Michael Dennis Browne
Full of Lust and Good Usage,
        Stephen Dunn (2nd edition)
Far and Away, Mark Jarman
Anniversary of the Air, Michael Waters
To the House Ghost, Paula Rankin
Midwinter Transport, Anne Bromley

1986
Seals in the Inner Harbor, Brendan Galvin
Thomas and Beulah, Rita Dove
Further Adventures With You, C.D. Wright
Fifteen to Infinity, Ruth Fainlight
False Statements, Jim Hall
When There Are No Secrets, C.G. Hanzlicek

1987
Some Gangster Pain, Gillian Conoley
Other Children, Lawrence Raab
Internal Geography, Richard Harteis
The Van Gogh Notebook, Peter Cooley

A Circus of Needs,
        Stephen Dunn, (second edition)
Ruined Cities, Vern Rutsala
Places and Stories, Kim R. Stafford

1988
Preparing to Be Happy, T. Alan Broughton
Red Letter Days, Mekeel McBride
The Abandoned Country, Thomas Rabbitt
The Book of Knowledge, Dara Wier
Changing the Name to Ochester, Ed Ochester
Weaving the Sheets, Judith Root

1989
Recital in a Private Home, Eve Shelnutt
A Walled Garden, Michael Cuddihy
The Age of Krypton, Carol J. Pierman
Land That Wasn't Ours, David Keller
Stations, Jay Meek
The Common Summer: New and Selected Poems,
        Robert Wallace
The Burden Lifters, Michael Waters
Falling Deeply into America, Gregory Djanikian
Entry in an Unknown Hand, Franz Wright

1990
Why the River Disappears, Marcia Southwick
Staying Up For Love, Leslie Adrienne Miller
Dreamer, Primus St. John

1991
Permanent Change, John Skoyles
Clackamas, Gary Gildner
Tall Stranger, Gillian Conoley
The Gathering of My Name, Cornelius Eady
A Dog in the Lifeboat, Joyce Peseroff
Raised Underground, Renate Wood
Divorce: A Romance, Paula Rankin

1992
Modern Ocean, James Harms
The Astonished Hours, Peter Cooley
You Won't Remember This, Michael Dennis Browne
Twenty Colors, Elizabeth Kirschner
First A Long Hesitation, Eve Shelnutt

Bountiful, Michael Waters
Blue for the Plough, Dara Wier
All That Heat in a Cold Sky, Elizabeth Libbey

1993
Trumpeter, Jeannine Savard
Cuba, Ricardo Pau-Llosa
The Night World and the Word Night, Franz Wright
The Book of Complaints, Richard Katrovas

1994
If Winter Come: Collected Poems, 1967–1992,
        Alvin Aubert
Of Desire and Disorder, Wayne Dodd
Ungodliness, Leslie Adrienne Miller
Rain, Henry Carlile
Windows, Jay Meek
A Handful of Bees, Dzvinia Orlowsky

1995
Germany, Caroline Finkelstein
Housekeeping in a Dream, Laura Kasischke
About Distance, Gregory Djanikian
Wind of the White Dresses, Mekeel McBride
Above the Tree Line, Kathy Mangan
In the Country of Elegies, T. Alan Broughton
Scenes from the Light Years, Anne C. Bromley
Quartet, Angela Ball
Rorschach Test, Franz Wright

1996
Back Roads, Patricia Henley
Dyer's Thistle, Peter Balakian
Beckon, Gillian Conoley
The Parable of Fire, James Reiss
Cold Pluto, Mary Ruefle
Orders of Affection, Arthur Smith
Colander, Michael McFee

1997
Growing Darkness, Growing Light, Jean Valentine
Selected Poems, 1965-1995, Michael Dennis Browne
Your Rightful Childhood: New and Selected Poems,
        Paula Rankin
Headlands: New and Selected Poems, Jay Meek

Soul Train, Allison Joseph
The Autobiography of a Jukebox, Cornelius Eady
The Patience of the Cloud Photographer,
        Elizabeth Holmes
Madly in Love, Aliki Barnstone
An Octave Above Thunder: New and Selected Poems, Carol Muske

1998
Yesterday Had a Man In It, Leslie Adrienne Miller
Definition of the Soul, John Skoyles
Dithyrambs, Richard Katrovas
Postal Routes, Elizabeth Kirschner
The Blue Salvages, Wayne Dodd
The Joy Addict, James Harms
Clemency and Other Poems, Colette Inez
Scattering the Ashes, Jeff Friedman
Sacred Conversations, Peter Cooley
Life Among the Trolls, Maura Stanton

1999
Justice, Caroline Finkelstein
Edge of House, Dzvinia Orlowsky
A Thousand Friends of Rain: New and Selected Poems, 1976-1998,
        Kim Stafford
The Devil's Child, Fleda Brown Jackson
World as Dictionary, Jesse Lee Kercheval
Vereda Tropical, Ricardo Pau-Llosa
The Museum of the Revolution, Angela Ball
Our Master Plan, Dara Wier

2000
Small Boat with Oars of Different Size, Thom Ward
Post Meridian, Mary Ruefle
Hierarchies of Rue, Roger Sauls
Constant Longing, Dennis Sampson
Mortal Education, Joyce Peseroff
How Things Are, James Richardson
Years Later, Gregory Djanikian
On the Waterbed They Sank to Their Own Levels,
        Sarah Rosenblatt
Blue Jesus, Jim Daniels
Winter Morning Walks: 100 Postcards to Jim Harrison,
        Ted Kooser

2001
The Deepest Part of the River, Mekeel McBride
The Origin of Green, T. Alan Broughton
Day Moon, Jon Anderson
Glacier Wine, Maura Stanton
Earthly, Michael McFee
Lovers in the Used World, Gillian Conoley
Ten Thousand Good Mornings, James Reiss
The World's Last Night, Margot Schilpp
Mastodon, 80% Complete, Jonathan Johnson
The Sex Lives of the Poor and Obscure, David Schloss
Voyages in English, Dara Wier
Quarters, James Harms

2002
Astronaut, Brian Henry
Among the Musk Ox People, Mary Ruefle
The Finger Bone, Kevin Prufer
Keeping Time, Suzanne Cleary
From the Book of Changes, Stephen Tapscott
What It Wasn't, Laura Kasischke
The Late World, Arthur Smith
Slow Risen Among the Smoke Trees, Elizabeth Kirschner

2003
Imitation of Life, Allison Joseph
A Place Made of Starlight, Peter Cooley
The Mastery Impulse, Ricardo Pau-Llosa
Except for One Obscene Brushstroke, Dzvinia Orlowsky
Taking Down the Angel, Jeff Friedman
Casino of the Sun, Jerry Williams
Trouble, Mary Baine Campbell
Lives of Water, John Hoppenthaler